STARFISH AQUAFARMING

Cultivating Starfish For Educational And Decorative Purposes

Enter The Unique World Of Starfish Farming For Aquariums, Research, And Educational Displays

Dr. Fabian Felicity

Table of Contents

CHAPTER ONE

Introduction

In the vast and intricate world of aquaculture, where innovation and sustainability are essential, an intriguing concept has emerged: starfish aquafarming. This unique method for cultivating starfish produces an unusual blend of marine biology, environmental awareness, and economic viability.

In this trip, we will delve into the interesting world of Starfish Aquafarming, learning about its appeal, benefits, and the processes required for a successful venture.

Why Starfish?

The choice to cultivate starfish stems from a combination of ecological and economic factors. Starfish, often known as sea stars, play a crucial role in marine ecosystems by encouraging biodiversity and maintaining population balance with other marine organisms.

Using the potential of starfish aquafarming might give a sustainable alternative to traditional aquaculture operations, therefore contributing to the conservation of marine ecosystems.

Furthermore, starfish possess unique biological characteristics that make them perfect for aquaculture.

Their regeneration capabilities, adaptability to a wide range of environments, and minimal maintenance requirements make them an attractive and practical option for aqua farmers. Understanding the appeal of starfish farming offers new avenues for sustainable aquaculture.

Getting Started

Starfish aquaculture requires careful planning and execution. Essential preliminary activities provide the groundwork for a successful venture by ensuring that the aquafarm is properly prepared to grow and sustain a healthy starfish population.

The first crucial step is to choose an appropriate location for the aquafarm. Considerations like water quality, temperature, and accessibility are important to the success of the venture. The chosen area should provide optimal conditions for starfish growth and development while also enabling efficient farm management processes.

After the space has been purchased, the next step is to create an adequate aquaculture system. This system must fulfill the unique needs of starfish, including water flow, filtration, and tank architecture. Attention to accuracy in system design results in a controlled environment that promotes the health and well-being of farmed stars.

Water quality management is crucial in starfish aquaculture. Regular monitoring of salinity, pH, and nutrient levels is essential to provide an environment conducive to starfish growth. Implementing adequate water treatment processes and maintaining optimal conditions are crucial to the aquafarm's overall effectiveness.

Selecting Starfish Species

Selecting the appropriate starfish species is critical to successful aquaculture. There are several species of starfish, each with its own set of characteristics and requirements. Understanding the specific needs of different starfish species is crucial for running a healthy and productive aquafarm.

Some starfish species are more resistant to changes in environmental conditions, making them ideal for aquaculture in a range of habitats. Others may have specific nutritional needs, demanding a thorough assessment of available food sources on the aquafarm.

Aquaculturists may increase their overall performance and productivity by selecting starfish species that are appropriate for the aquafarm's natural circumstances and resources.

In addition to environmental compatibility, market demand for certain starfish species must be addressed. Identifying species that are in high demand in the aquaculture business ensures the venture's financial success.

This careful selection technique in starfish aquaculture strikes a compromise between environmental sustainability and commercial profitability.

In the continuously changing aquaculture landscape, Starfish Aquafarming stands out as a promising and innovative technique. Aquafarmers may embark on a path to sustainable and financially viable production by understanding the ecological significance of starfish, using their unique biological qualities, and implementing precise planning.

The appeal of starfish aquafarming arises not just from its potential to benefit marine conservation, but also from its ability to supply a lucrative and marketable commodity.

As the world seeks sustainable solutions in a multitude of areas, starfish aquafarming stands out as a beacon of hope, offering a harmonious combination of environmental responsibility and economic success.

CHAPTER TWO
Aquarium Setup: Creating An Ideal Environment For Starfish Cultivation

In the realm of aquaculture, successful starfish growth is heavily reliant on the creation of an optimal aquarium habitat. Creating the appropriate environment is essential for satisfying the special needs of these fascinating aquatic creatures.

Every aspect, from aquarium size and kind to substrate and décor choices, is important to the health and growth of mature starfish.

Choosing The Appropriate Aquarium Size And Kind

Choosing the appropriate size and kind of aquarium is the first step in creating a perfect environment for starfish growth.

Larger tanks are often favored since they allow for more movement and mimic the diverse surroundings that starfish are used to in nature. The design of the aquarium is also important since circular or oval forms encourage better water circulation.

Specific starfish species need inquiry into their natural environmental conditions. Some may thrive in rocky circumstances, while others need sandy soil. Matching the aquarium type to the starfish species' needs is critical for their overall health and productivity.

Creating A Suitable Substrate And Décor

The substrate and décor of the aquarium help to recreate the natural habitat of starfish. Most starfish species flourish on sand or fine gravel surfaces, which mimic the sandy ocean bottoms where these organisms might be found.

Incorporating rocks and live corals increases the looks while also providing hiding places and surfaces for attachment.

The furnishings should highlight both the aquarium's visual appeal and the starfish's comfort. Avoid utilizing sharp or abrasive things that might harm the delicate bodies of these aquatic organisms.

Furthermore, offering a diversity of structures, such as caverns and fissures, allows starfish to explore and find sanctuary.

Feeding And Nutrition: Understanding Starfish Dietary Needs In Aquaculture

Proper nutrition is critical for the health and vitality of farmed starfish. Understanding the nutritional needs of these marine invertebrates is essential for developing a feeding strategy that promotes growth and overall well-being. Starfish are omnivores, consuming both live and frozen foods.

Identifying Suitable Starfish Diet

Starfish eat a variety of animals in their natural habitat, including small fish, mollusks, and detritus. In aquaculture, replicating this diverse diet is crucial for meeting nutritional requirements.

Commercially available starfish food, which includes brine shrimp, plankton, and other marine animals, is an easy method to provide a well-balanced diet.

Starfish may be given live foods such as small shrimp or clams to improve their natural hunting abilities. It is vital to evaluate each starfish species' feeding habits and adjust their diet accordingly to ensure they get the nutrients they need for growth and reproduction.

CHAPTER THREE

Water Quality Management: Creating Ideal Conditions For Starfish Health And Growth

Maintaining excellent water quality in the aquarium is critical for successful starfish growth. Temperature, salinity, pH, and nutrient levels are all significant variables to consider while regulating water quality.

Maintaining these components within an optimal range is crucial for cultured starfish health, growth, and reproduction.

Balancing Temperature And Salinity

Starfish are quite sensitive to temperature and salinity variations, thus it is vital to keep the tank conditions steady. Most starfish species prefer a temperature range of 72°F to 78°F, with salt levels between 32 and 35 parts per thousand (ppt) in the marine environment. Regular monitoring and revisions are essential to prevent stress and health problems caused by changes in these factors.

Managing Ph And Nutrient Content

Starfish need a stable pH level to operate correctly. The optimal pH range is usually between 8.0 and 8.4.

To prevent acidic or alkaline conditions that might kill starfish, pH buffers must be tested and changed regularly.

Monitoring nutrient levels, particularly ammonia, nitrite, and nitrate, is as critical as pH. Ammonia and nitrite levels should be kept undetectable, while nitrate levels should be controlled by regular water changes and the use of biological filtration devices.

Proper Methods For Handling And Caring For Farmed Starfish

To avoid stress and potential harm, farmed starfish must be handled and cared for with a soft touch and exact abilities. Whether it's routine maintenance or addressing specific health issues, taking the appropriate precautions is crucial to the life of these marine creatures.

Gentle Handling Techniques

To avoid causing injury to the starfish, handle it gently. Starfish have a unique water vascular system that enables them to move and control their tube feet. These delicate structures must be handled with care to prevent damage. When removing a starfish from an aquarium for cleaning or relocation, a soft net or cupping technique may assist in lessening stress.

CHAPTER FOUR

Monitoring And Early Identification Of Health Issues

Regular inspections of farmed starfish are essential for early detection of health issues. Color, demeanor, and the appearance of lesions may indicate underlying concerns.

Prompt actions, like isolating sick individuals or altering water conditions, may assist in preventing disease propagation and protecting starfish health.

Breeding And Reproduction: Understanding Starfish Reproductive Processes In Aquafarming

Understanding starfish reproductive processes is crucial for successful aquaculture breeding. Unlike many other marine species, starfish may reproduce both sexually and asexually. Proper breeding procedures may increase the viability of starfish cultivation attempts.

Sexual And Asexual Reproduction In Starfish

Starfish are known for their remarkable ability to regenerate, which is closely linked to their reproductive activity. Sexual reproduction involves the release of eggs and sperm into water for external fertilization, while asexual reproduction occurs when missing biological components are regenerated.

Creating favorable conditions for sexual reproduction includes maintaining a healthy population with enough nutrition and stable environmental conditions. It is also vital to provide enough space and appropriate substrates for spawning to ensure successful breeding.

Finally, growing starfish in aquafarming requires careful consideration of a wide range of issues, including tank design, feeding, water quality management, handling, and reproduction. Understanding and adhering to these critical factors enables aquafarmers to establish an environment that promotes the health, growth, and reproductive success of generated starfish, so ensuring the survival of this unique and exciting marine species.

Educational Applications: Utilizing Cultivated Starfish For Displays And Research

Starfish have become popular themes in marine teaching and research, providing a unique opportunity to involve both students and experts. Cultivating starfish for educational and scientific purposes has grown in favor in recent years, offering a hands-on approach to learning about marine life and ecosystems.

Educational Displays As A Learning Tool

Educational exhibitions using farmed starfish are great tools for teaching marine biology. Starfish, with their complex structure and varied behaviors, pique the curiosity of students at all educational levels. Whether in basic schools or advanced research institutions, the tactile sense of seeing and handling these aquatic species enhances the learning experience.

These exhibitions often include interactive elements that allow youngsters to explore the anatomy of starfish via touch and observation. Real-time displays of feeding habits, motility, and reproduction contribute to our general understanding of marine life.

The tactile nature of these displays piques curiosity and fosters a greater connection to the subject matter.

CHAPTER FIVE
Research Opportunities And Scientific Inquiry

Beyond instructive displays, rearing starfish provides several opportunities for scientific research. Understanding starfish physiology, genetics, and ecological roles helps us better understand marine ecosystems in general.

Researchers may investigate how environmental factors impact starfish health, behavior, and reproduction, giving insights into the intricate dynamics of ocean life.

Cultivated starfish offer a controlled environment for investigating their life cycles and responses to various stimuli. This controlled setting enables researchers to conduct experiments that would be difficult or impossible in the wild. As a result, the results of this research have the potential to boost conservation efforts and improve the overall health of marine ecosystems.

Decorative Displays: Improving Aesthetics With Starfish In Aquariums And Exhibitions

Starfish are fascinating not just for instructional purposes, but also for adding to the beauty of aquariums and displays. Adding farmed starfish to decorative displays increases their visual appeal and immersive experience for visitors.

Aesthetic Contributions To Aquariums

Aquariums, with their diverse marine life, aim to capture the beauty and complexity of underwater habitats. Cultivated starfish, with their vibrant colors and intricate patterns, provide a sense of beauty to these artificial habitats. Their presence adds to the overall aesthetic appeal, resulting in visually stunning exhibitions that catch the attention of aquarium visitors.

Strategically placing starfish in aquarium settings provides for a variety of viewing angles, emphasizing their attractive qualities. The juxtaposition of their vibrant hues against the backdrop of coral reefs and aquatic flora creates a visually striking image. As a consequence, starfish not only add to the educational value of aquariums, but they also serve as living artworks that enrich the overall visual experience.

Immersive Displays Provide Compelling Experiences.

Larger exhibits and immersive works use farmed starfish, offering visitors with a multimodal experience. These exhibits go beyond traditional aquarium displays, providing settings that imitate starfish's natural habitats. Visitors may experience firsthand how starfish interact with other aquatic animals, raising awareness of the interconnectedness of marine ecosystems.

The immersive aspect of these exhibits extends beyond visual engagement. Visitors may be able to touch and interact with starfish while being supervised by expert professionals, enhancing the whole experience. Such hands-on encounters leave an everlasting impression, establishing a sense of wonder and connectedness to the aquatic world.

Challenges And Solutions: Addressing Common Challenges In Starfish Aquaculture

While raising starfish for educational and decorative purposes has many benefits, it is not without drawbacks. Addressing common challenges in starfish aquaculture is crucial for ensuring the marine creatures' long-term survival and health.

Environmental Concerns

One of the most challenging parts of starfish aquaculture is replicating the complicated and delicate balance of their natural surroundings. Cultivated starfish need optimal water quality, temperature, and nourishment to grow. Environmental monitoring systems and advanced filtering technologies help to mitigate these concerns by establishing a controlled environment that resembles ocean conditions.

Health And Disease Management

Another concern in starfish aquaculture is disease susceptibility, which may affect the whole colony. Close monitoring of the health of adult starfish is necessary to identify and prevent any outbreaks immediately. Strict quarantine measures, regular health exams, and preventive treatments all contribute to maintaining a healthy and disease-free populace.

Conclusion: Celebrating The Success And Joy Of Cultivating Starfish

To conclude, the cultivation of starfish for educational displays, research, and visually appealing exhibits is a harmonic combination of science, education, and art. The versatility of these marine organisms makes them ideal for engaging pupils, enhancing scientific knowledge, and improving the visual appeal of aquatic environments.

The educational applications of farmed starfish not only enrich the learning experience but also develop a sense of responsibility for marine conservation. These exhibitions inspire a new generation of environmental stewards who are committed to preserving the health and diversity of our oceans by revealing the complexity of marine life.

The use of farmed starfish in aquariums and exhibits improves their visual appeal, transforming them into immersive experiences that engage and educate guests. The combination of art and science in such displays creates a dynamic and fascinating experience that highlights the beauty and complexity of marine ecosystems.

While there are challenges in starfish aquaculture, new ideas, and technical advancements are paving the way for more sustainable practices. By addressing environmental problems, health management, and other difficulties, starfish cultivation may thrive, ensuring that these lovely creatures continue to amaze and educate future generations.

Celebrating the success and enjoyment of starfish cultivation displays not just human innovation, but also a commitment to preserving the gems that exist in our seas.

* 9 7 9 8 8 7 9 5 3 0 9 6 4 *